The United States Constitution and the Bill of Rights

The Law of the Land

Anna Keegan

NEW YORK

Published in 2016 by The Rosen Publishing Group, Inc.
29 East 21st Street, New York, NY 10010

Photo Credits: Cover SuperStock/Getty Images; p. 4 Universal Images Group/Getty Images; pp. 5, 12–13, 17 National Archives and Records Administration; p. 6 © H. Armstrong Roberts/ClassicStock/The Image Works; p. 7 Hulton Archive/Getty Images; p. 9 DEA Picture Library/De Agostini/Getty Images; p. 11 Publications.USA.gov; p. 15 Library of Congress Prints and Photographs Division; p. 19 State Library and Archives of Florida; p. 20 © North Wind Picture Archives; p. 21 Underwood Archives/Archive Photos/Getty Images.

Library of Congress Cataloging-in-Publication Data

Keegan, Anna.
The United States Constitution and the Bill of Rights : the law of the land / Anna Keegan. -- First edition.
    pages cm. -- (Spotlight on Aamerican history)
Includes index.
ISBN 978-1-4994-1777-7 (library bound) -- ISBN 978-1-4994-1773-9 (pbk.) -- ISBN 978-1-4994-1771-5 (6-pack)
1. United States. Constitution--Juvenile literature. 2. United States--Politics and government--1775-1783--Juvenile literature. 3. United States--Politics and government--1783-1789--Juvenile literature. 4. Constitutional history--United States--Juvenile literature. I. Title.
E303.K44 2016
342.7302'9--dc23
                        2015024481

Manufactured in the United States of America

CPSIA Compliance Information: Batch #WS15PK: For Further Information contact Rosen Publishing, New York, New York at 1-800-237-9932

CONTENTS

THE DOCUMENT THAT DEFINED A NATION

By the end of the American Revolutionary War, the new American nation needed a new body of law. Patriots had fought and died to be free of the tyranny of the British king and the unfair laws of his **Parliament**. Americans had won the right to govern themselves. They were now free to create their own democratic government. This government would be

General George Washington led his Continental army to victory against the British in the American War of Independence. In this painting, General Washington rides in triumph through the streets of Boston.

The original handwritten and signed copy of the Constitution of the United States lives at the National Archives in Washington, D.C.

for the people and by the people. The people of the United States could elect their leaders. Americans wanted to make sure that no one in government became so strong that he or she could ignore what the people wanted.

The United States Constitution became law in 1787. It states how the United States government works. For the first time in history, the powers of a central government were limited. The Bill of Rights was added to the Constitution in 1791. It protects the personal rights of **citizens**, such as freedom of speech and religious choice.

THE ARTICLES OF CONFEDERATION

The Second Continental Congress (1776–1777) created the first set of laws that governed the original 13 states. This body of law was called the Articles of Confederation. It was ratified, or approved, by all 13 states in 1781. Each state still wanted to keep a lot of power for itself. This made the central government very weak. The congress could make decisions, but it did not have the power to make states do what it

In this painting of the Second Continental Congress, members vote for independence on July 4, 1776.

In this engraving we see George Washington leading the Constitutional Convention. The convention was in Philadelphia, Pennsylvania. It ran from May 25 to September 17, 1787.

decided. The government had very little money. It needed to ask the states for money. States were not paying their taxes. As a result, the government had trouble paying the soldiers who had fought in the Revolutionary War.

Important leaders of the Revolution such as George Washington and Benjamin Franklin feared that the country might not survive. Something had to be done. American leaders held a meeting in Philadelphia, Pennsylvania, to talk about ways to solve these problems. The meeting is now known as the Constitutional Convention.

THE CONSTITUTIONAL CONVENTION

The Constitutional Convention took place in Philadelphia, Pennsylvania, from May 14 to September 17, 1787. **Delegates** from 12 of the 13 states attended the convention. Only Rhode Island decided not to come, as it feared the new laws would not be in the state's best interests.

At first, the delegates to the convention wanted only to improve the Articles of Confederation, but James Madison of Virginia and Alexander Hamilton of New York believed strongly that there should be a new set of laws and a new government. The rest of the delegates soon agreed with this. They elected George Washington as president of the convention.

There were many debates about different issues. There were many versions of the wording of each article, or law. Finally the delegates succeeded at creating the Constitution of the United States. Thirty-eight delegates from 12 states signed the document. The document then went to each state for approval by special state conventions. Only nine states needed to approve the Constitution to make it the law

This 18th-century painting allows us to witness a historic moment. Here we see delegates signing the Constitution in 1787.

of the land. On June 21, 1788, New Hampshire became the ninth state to approve the Constitution.

The **preamble** of the Constitution explains why the delegates worked so hard to create the Constitution. Their goal was "to form a more perfect union."

9

THE THREE BRANCHES OF GOVERNMENT

The Constitution is a social contract between the people and the government. The government gives people things they cannot give to themselves. These things include justice, peace, and defense from enemies.

The Constitution has seven articles that explain the laws under which the government works. The first three articles explain the three branches of government. These branches create a system of checks and balances. Each branch keeps the others in check so that one branch doesn't become too powerful.

Article I describes the legislative branch, or Congress, which makes the laws. Congress is made up of the Senate and the House of Representatives. Article I establishes how elections happen. It establishes the qualifications of members of Congress. Section 8 of Article I lists the powers of the legislative branch. These include collecting taxes and borrowing money.

Article II covers the executive branch. This describes the powers of the president of the United States. The president is the head of the executive branch. This article also describes the powers of the

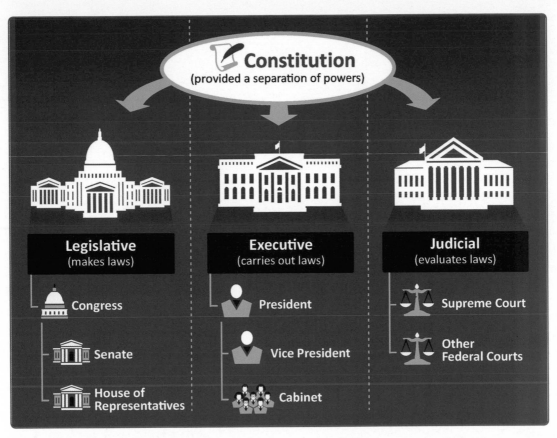

This chart was created by the United States government. It shows the three branches of government and the separation of powers.

vice president. Section 2 of Article II, for example, describes the president's role as commander in chief of the military. The president can makes treaties with help from the Senate.

Article III explains how the judicial branch works. This includes the **Supreme Court**. Article III describes how legal decisions are made. It protects citizens by ensuring a trial by **jury** for criminal cases. It also **defines** what **treason** is.

September 3, 1783

The Treaty of Paris is signed, ending the American Revolution.

September 17, 1787

After months of debate, 39 delegates sign the Constitution.

1782   1783   1784   1785   1786   1787

May 25, 1787

The Constitutional Convention starts in Philadelphia.

KEY DATES ON THE ROAD TO RATIFICATION

April 30, 1789

George Washington becomes the first president of the United States of America.

December 15, 1791

Virginia becomes the tenth and final state needed to ratify the Bill of Rights.

1788   1789   1790   1791   1792   1793

June 21, 1788

New Hampshire ratifies the Constitution, making it the law of the land.

May 29, 1790

Rhode Island becomes the thirteenth and final state to ratify the Constitution.

FINAL ARTICLES OF THE LAW OF THE LAND

Articles IV to VI of the Constitution set rules that each state must follow, explain how changes can be made to the Constitution, and establish that the Constitution is the supreme law of the land.

It was important to the writers of the Constitution that the federal government had enough power over the states that it could govern them. Article IV sets rules that each state must follow. It explains how new states can join the Union. It requires that all states must honor the laws of the other states. It also explains the relationship between the federal government and the states. Article IV also prevents state governments from **discriminating** against the citizens of other states. Finally, Article IV requires that the federal government must protect the states in times of war.

The writers of the Constitution realized that over time, the government might need to make changes to the Constitution. These changes are called amendments. Article V explains the process that must be followed for amendments to be made to the Constitution.

This political cartoon was created in 1787. It shows deep divisions in Connecticut politics over the ratification of the United States Constitution. The wagon is a symbol for Connecticut. It is sinking slowly into the mud.

Article VI states that the Constitution is the supreme, or highest, law of the land. It demands that all judges must follow the laws of the Constitution. It also states that no person running for public office shall have to pass a religious test. Article VI also sets the rule that only nine states are needed to ratify the Constitution for it to become law. This happened when New Hampshire ratified the Constitution on June 21, 1788.

TEN AMENDMENTS: THE BILL OF RIGHTS

Soon after the Constitution became the law of the land, James Madison drafted 12 amendments to the Constitution. Article V of the Constitution allows for this. Of these 12 amendments, 10 became the Bill of Rights. These 10 amendments are very specific about individual liberty and justice.

The First Amendment guarantees religious freedom. It says that citizens may worship as they wish. The First Amendment also states that citizens may also say or write what they want and may meet peacefully in groups. This amendment states that citizens may make complaints to the government.

James Madison believed strongly that the country needed a national guard, or **militia**, for protection. The Second Amendment gives citizens the right to bear, or carry, arms or guns.

The Third Amendment says that citizens do not have to house soldiers in their homes unless the government makes a special law during a war. This amendment was created because citizens had very fresh memories of British soldiers living in Americans' homes before the Revolution.

Congress of the United States,

begun and held at the City of New-York, on

Wednesday the fourth of March, one thousand seven hundred and eighty-nine.

THE Conventions of a number of the States, having at the time of their adopting the Constitution, expressed a desire, in order to prevent misconstruction or abuse of its powers, that further declaratory and restrictive clauses should be added: And as extending the ground of public confidence in the Government, will best ensure the beneficent ends of its institution.

RESOLVED by the Senate and House of Representatives of the United States of America, in Congress assembled, two thirds of both Houses concurring, that the following Articles be proposed to the Legislatures of the several States, as amendments to the Constitution of the United States, all, or any of which Articles, when ratified by three fourths of the said Legislatures, to be valid to all intents and purposes, as part of the said Constitution, viz.

ARTICLES in addition to, and amendment of the Constitution of the United States of America, proposed by Congress, and ratified by the Legislatures of the several States, pursuant to the fifth Article of the original Constitution.

Article the first..... After the first enumeration required by the first Article of the Constitution, there shall be one Representative for every thirty thousand, until the number shall amount to one hundred, after which, the proportion shall be so regulated by Congress, that there shall be not less than one hundred Representatives, nor less than one Representative for every forty thousand persons, until the number of Representatives shall amount to two hundred, after which the proportion shall be so regulated by Congress, that there shall not be less than two hundred Representatives, nor more than one Representative for every fifty thousand persons.

Article the second... No law, varying the compensation for the services of the Senators and Representatives, shall take effect, until an election of Representatives shall have intervened.

Article the third... Congress shall make no law respecting an establishment of religion, or prohibiting the free exercise thereof; or abridging the freedom of speech, or of the press; or the right of the people peaceably to assemble, and to petition the Government for a redress of grievances.

Article the fourth... A well regulated Militia, being necessary to the security of a free State, the right of the people to keep and bear arms, shall not be infringed.

Article the fifth...... No Soldier shall, in time of peace be quartered in any house, without the consent of the owner, nor in time of war, but in a manner to be prescribed by law.

Article the sixth..... The right of the people to be secure in their persons, houses, papers, and effects, against unreasonable searches and seizures, shall not be violated, and no Warrants shall issue, but upon probable cause, supported by oath or affirmation, and particularly describing the place to be searched, and the persons or things to be seized.

Article the seventh... No person shall be held to answer for a capital, or otherwise infamous crime, unless on a presentment or indictment of a Grand Jury, except in cases arising in the land or naval forces, or in the Militia, when in actual service in time of War or public danger; nor shall any person be subject for the same offence to be twice put in jeopardy of life or limb; nor shall be compelled in any criminal case to be a witness against himself, nor be deprived of life, liberty, or property, without due process of law; nor shall private property be taken for public use, without just compensation.

Article the eighth... In all criminal prosecutions, the accused shall enjoy the right to a speedy and public trial, by an impartial jury of the State and district wherein the crime shall have been committed, which district shall have been previously ascertained by law, and to be informed of the nature and cause of the accusation; to be confronted with the witnesses against him; to have compulsory process for obtaining witnesses in his favor, and to have the assistance of counsel for his defence.

Article the ninth... In suits at common law, where the value in controversy shall exceed twenty dollars, the right of trial by jury shall be preserved, and no fact tried by a jury, shall be otherwise re-examined in any Court of the United States, than according to the rules of the common law.

Article the tenth...

Article the eleventh...

Article the twelfth...

ATTEST,

John Beckley, Clerk of the

_____ Secretary of the Senate.

The Fourth Amendment states that the police cannot arrest citizens or search their homes without a warrant, or approval, from a judge.

The Fifth Amendment protects the rights of citizens accused of crimes.

The Sixth Amendment guarantees citizens the right to a **lawyer** and a fair trial by jury.

The Seventh Amendment guarantees that if one citizen sues another for more than $20, that person has the right to a trial by jury.

The Eighth Amendment states that all fines and punishments for crimes must be fair.

The Ninth Amendment states that citizens may have other rights that must also be protected.

The Tenth Amendment states that powers not specifically given to the federal government belong to the states.

INSTITUTION STATE PENITENTARY RAIFORDI. CELL NUMBER D-9

NAME CLARENCE EARL GIDEON NUMBER 003826

SUPHREME COURT
STATE OF FLORIDA

PETITION FOR WRIT OF HABEUS CORPUS

Deny

I Clarence Earl Gideon, informs
This court that I am a pauper with
out funds ore any possiblty of
obtaining financeble aid and I Beg
of this court to listen and act
upon my plea

2: On the 3rd day of June 1961
A.D. I was arrested and charged
with the crime of Breaking and
entering with the intent to
commit a misdeamer to wit
petty Larceny. And that I plead
not guilty to this charge. That

The landmark case of *Gideon v. Wainwright* (1963) upheld the Sixth
Amendment's guarantee that citizens have a right to a lawyer in a trial. Seen
above is Earl Gideon's petition to the Supreme Court. Because he was denied a
lawyer in his trial, the Supreme Court reversed the lower court's decision.

LATER AMENDMENTS

The Bill of Rights was created to protect citizens' rights. Laws, however, are a product of the times in which they are created. The Founding Fathers who drafted the Constitution had a specific definition of who was a citizen. It would be many years before the government treated all people, no matter their race or gender, equally under the law.

In this hand-colored woodcut, African American men are shown voting in Richmond, Virginia, in 1871.

This photograph from 1920 shows women in New York City lining up to vote for the first time. The passage of the Nineteenth Amendment allowed them to do so.

In 1865, the Thirteenth Amendment outlawed slavery. In 1868, the Fourteenth Amendment promised American citizens of all races equal protection under the law. In 1870, the Fifteenth Amendment stated that no man could be refused the right to vote based on race, color, or the fact that he had once been a slave. In 1920, women finally won the right to vote when Tennessee became the final state needed to ratify the Nineteenth Amendment.

A MODEL
FOR FREEDOM

Before the ratification of the Constitution in 1787, many people could not imagine a nation not ruled by a king. The idea of a country created by the people and for the people was a revolutionary idea. Today most of the countries of the world are governed under the laws of a constitution. These constitutions were inspired and influenced by the United States Constitution. We can see this influence in the French Constitution of 1791 and the Constitution of Nigeria in 1999.

The U.S. Constitution is a living document. It changes and grows as new amendments are proposed and passed. Currently there are 27 amendments. The twenty-sixth, for example, was added in 1971. It lowered the legal voting age to 18. At seven articles and 27 amendments, the U.S. Constitution is the shortest written constitution currently being used. The Constitution and the Bill of Rights are the purest expression of what it means to live in the United States of America.

GLOSSARY

citizens (SIH-tih-zenz) People who are born in or who have the legal right to live in a certain country.

defines (de-FYNZ) Explains the meaning of a word.

delegates (DE-li-guhts) People who are chosen to vote or act for others.

discriminating (duh-skrih-muh-NAY-ting) Unfairly treating a person or group of people differently from other people or groups of people.

jury (JUHR-ree) A group of people who are members of the public and are chosen to make a decision in a legal case.

lawyer (LOY-yuhr) A person whose job is to guide and assist people in matters relating to the law.

militia (muh-LIH-shuh) A group of people who are trained like soldiers.

Parliament (PAHR-luh-muhnt) The group of people in England who are responsible for making the country's laws.

preamble (PREE-am-buhl) A statement that is made at the beginning of something.

Supreme Court (SOO-preem KORT) The highest court of the United States.

treason (TREE-zuhn) The crime of trying to overthrow your country's government or of helping your country's enemies during war.

INDEX

PRIMARY SOURCE LIST

Page 4: *George Washington Riding In Triumph*, chromolithograph from 1879, artist unknown.

Page 6: *Congress Voting the Declaration of Independence*, oil painting. This painting was started in 1784 by Robert Edge Pine (1730–1788). It was finished in 1801 by Edward Savage (1761–1817).

Page 15: *The Looking Glass for 1787. A House Divided Against Itself Cannot Stand. Mat. Chap. 13th, Verse 26*, by Amos Doolittle (1754–1832). This cartoon is an engraving with watercolor paint on laid paper, created in 1787, New Haven, Connecticut. Laid paper was hand-made in a wood press, and had a finely ribbed surface.

Page 19: Image of the first page of a hand-written Petition for Writ of Habeas Corpus by Clarence Earl Gideon. Gideon was a prison inmate who filed a lawsuit against the Secretary of the Florida Department of Corrections. The Writ is stored in the Florida Supreme Court Case Files, S. 49, Box 2780, Case 31116.

Page 20: Antique woodcut by William L. Sheppard (1833– 1912). This woodcut was originally published in *Frank Leslie's Illustrated Newspaper*, New York, 1871.

Page 21: Original photograph of female citizens voting for the first time in 1920, in New York City. Photographer unknown.

WEBSITES

Due to the changing nature of Internet links, PowerKids Press has developed an online list of websites related to the subject of this book. This site is updated regularly. Please use this link to access the list: www.powerkidslinks.com/soah/bill